DREAMS

A collection of short poems

By

Keith Hearn

ISBN-13 978-1974308972
ISBN – 10: 1974308979

Acknowledgements

I find writing poetry relaxing and it makes me feel extremely calm

I hope when reading the poetry, you will find one that will resonate with someone

Poetry is a personal thing

DREAMS

ENJOY

<u>SHANGRI LA</u>

Is it so wrong to want to live in peace?

To shut the violence and hatred from
one another's minds

We don't live in Shangri la we
regrettably live in the real world

The world at this moment in time is
run by people who seem hell bent on
leading the people of the world to the
very brink of destruction

Man is destroying the natural world
and have turned their attention to
wanting to destroy mankind

<u>*THOUGHTS*</u>

The thought of you is constantly on my mind

Thoughts of you run around my head

Whenever I see another woman my thoughts drift towards you and to what I miss most in life

I wonder many a time to what you are doing

Do you also think the same things as I do?

Who knows

<u>*WHAT IF*</u>

Why, oh why won't you meet me?

It is the only way to get to know one
another

To not to meet is only denying yourself
a happy future

By denying yourself the opportunity to
find true happiness will only make you
think later in life "what if"

If it is your wish to live with the
biggest regret you will ever make then
that is your decision to make and not
mine

DREAMS

To deny yourself such happiness is very sad

<u>*HAPPENING*</u>

*Sometimes what you really want in life
is only hand shake away but it might
as well be miles away*

My own life at present feels like that

*I suppose in my mind it is never going
to happen*

*I have spent so much of my own life on
my own and have learnt how to block
people from entering my life*

But this is not how I want things to be

<u>YOU AND LIFE</u>

*I have always dreamt about you being
so close to me*

*To enjoy having your company on our
journey through life*

*To share the ups and downs and to
pick one another up when things in
life get too much*

*My life would be complete with you in
my life*

*To wake up with you besides me would
make my day feel just perfect*

OUTSIDE

You come across as a kind and loving
person
Your soft words and actions sometimes
come across as a little quirky

A loving heart beats just like a big,
base, drum

Your dog's love you without favour

You walk on the common in your bare
feet to feel mother earth beneath your
feet

You try your best to explore the
outside world to overcome your angst

DREAMS

*You try to show others your world
through the camera lens*

FIELDS

The rolling fields are laid out as far as
the eye can see

Row upon row of patchwork fields of
all colours and hews

There are fields covered in dark green,
light green, browns and yellow

A hopscotch of colours spread out and
dropping off in the distance

A tiny tractor in the far-off distance is
ploughing the many fields turning
them to a deep brown colour

Tilling the ancient land just like the
ancestors before

Ancient tracks cut alongside the fields
to allow access to the ancient land

As the farmer tills the fields, hundreds
of birds descend behind the tractor to
search for a morsel of food

The fields provide an abundance of
food for both mankind and wildlife

<u>*STRANGE*</u>

*Life can seem very strange even
stranger when on one's own*

*Life could be so much happier sharing
it with another*

*Life is so much easier if a problem is
shared with a loved one*

*Some may feel it is a cry for help to
need and want someone, possibly to
someone else a person who is far too
needy*

*Is it such a crime to want to share life
with another?*

HERMIT

Can someone really be a hermit
throughout their life?

To turn their back on the world and to
be cut off from life

To make the conscious decision to make
oneself unavailable to the rest of the
world it seems such a shame

Perhaps a person who wants to shut
themselves off from others could
impasse so much knowledge to others
who might learn as great deal

perhaps they have decided to live a hermit existence because having been deeply hurt be another person?

How sad to cut oneself off from the world?

<u>SHARING</u>

It is amazing when another person
opens an entirely different world own
which opens to so many shared
experiences

Gone is the insular world and because
my eyes have been opened to be able to
see a totally different world

Sharing one another's world seemed
alien and so strange at first

It is a world of give and take and it is
something that takes time to get used
to

SENSES

*The soft touch of your hand sent
shivers shooting down my spine*

*It had been such a long time since I
had felt the intimacy of another person*

The simplest of things mean so much

I was greedy and want more from you

*Life had been so bereft of the closeness
and the intimacy of another person*

KIND

*I have found kindness but nice and
kind don't seem to work in the world of
today*

*For every time I have been kind and
nice towards someone special it does
not seem to work*

*Those people didn't seem to want a
kind and loving person*

To them it is a form of weakness

*Perhaps I come across as someone is
needy*

DREAMS

There must be someone in need of a kind and loving person in their lives?

LIFE

Who and what are we? What is our purpose in this life of ours?

Surely, we are placed on this earth to enjoy life and to make some good while we are here

But as always along the journey of life thing don't always go according to plan

It is the point some people begin to become disillusioned and cynical about life and it is where their outlook on life becomes so disillusioned and very bitter

Some continue to feel bitter and twisted during their lifetime and others wish to do good in their own lives

Children's perspective on life is shaped by adults who have an influence on their world

<u>DREAM ON</u>

Dreams are formed in an individual's own mind

Their dreams may take decades to bear fruit sometimes their dreams are never fulfilled and remain locked away in their minds forever

Sometimes their dreams are resurrected with future generations and their dreams are see through other people

have a dream and to never let go of it, and to follow it through is one of the greatest feelings someone can have

It doesn't mean every dream leads to success but what it does mean the dream has been seen through and you have taken a chance and made a go of making it come true

Rest assured you have achieved the dream

No more what if's

LITTLE

How very pretty you look with your beautiful trestles cascading around your face

Your hair frames your features highlighting your olive skin

I could listen to your voice all day long

Your silver rings on your fingers glint in the light

But what has gone on in your past that has made you who you are?

DREAMS

Animals are your companions but who am I to judge

TIME

Time waits for no one

We all waste are time in life and look
back and think that we should have
done more with our lives and not to
have wasted so much time

That is until we find that there is no
time left to catch up on the things we
didn't do

But when that happens it is when we
realise we have finally ran out of time

Time waits for no one

WORDS

I sit at the bar thinking about my
dreams

Always dreaming of bettering myself
and to be someone

I only wish to try and do the simple
things in life

No everyone is so fortunate in life and
are happy with their lot

Words can portray to others another
world words are a portal to another
world

DREAMS

Some where they can imagine a fictional world through a writer's eyes

HOME

I am fully aware of how close I am to leaving my home to give up on my own dream

I have always envisaged living in my home until I die

Unfortunately, it is never going to happen

Time has finally run out on me

Things have a horrible habit of catching up and putting paid to the best laid plans

DREAMS

Life can be so cruel but as the well-known saying goes "that's life" and it sometimes sucks

INTEREST

I saw you from across the room and
your beauty took my breath away

Your eyes were sparkling in the light

You looked so radiant sitting with
your many friends

I didn't expect you to take any interest
in me

I was the last person I thought you
would be interested in

I thought my age would be a massive
barrier to you

DREAMS

Oh, how pretty your smile is your face
lit up when you smiled at me

As soon as our eyes locked together
your beaming smile won me over

STAR GAZING

The simple act of looking up at the
stars on a clear winter evening makes
me dream

I look up at the stars and think about
you and if you are doing the same
looking up at the stars in the sky

In London you are staring up at the
stars from within your small garden
and thinking the same thoughts as I

I once again gaze up to the stars
wishing for my dreams to come true

If only we weren't looking up at the stars on our own and instead looking at the stars together

DIFFERENT DREAMS

Others dream about all sorts of
different things in life

Be it the safe delivery of a new born

Or some may dream of their football
team winning the cup final, I know I
do

Some dream of doing well in their
chosen profession

We all have our own dreams

DREAMS

Dreams are so very personal and belong to no one else

It is of their choosing when they share their dreams with another person

Other people are only allowed to hear of another person's dreams when it feels just right or if the dream has come true

<u>A FAR AWAY LAND</u>

When I was a child living in a
faraway land I would often look up at
the night sky and think of what other
members of my family were up to at
that precise moment in time

I would think to myself what were
they doing while I was standing gazing
at the sky in a hot miserable land

Did they know how we were living in
such a place

Living in an extinct volcano in the
wilds of a desolate country

DREAMS

A I finished looking up at the stars it was soon time for bed

To face another day

THE EDGE

*It seems that throughout the world
there are those politicians on whatever
side of the political spectrum*

*who are pushing the wold to the very
brink of something very dark and
incompressible to even think about the
consequences are*

*Within less than a year the world has
changed so much*

*Man seems to want to destroy the
world we live in*

DREAMS

If humanity isn't careful mother nature herself will destroy herself and then there will be no way back

<u>WORKING UNTIL DEATH</u>

So many people work until they drop

Then when their working life is at an end they are unable to enjoy life to the full

Their very being has been drained of life

While working they are chasing the dollar thinking as soon as they have earnt enough they can buy themselves lasting happiness

They dream about what many people take for granted

DREAMS

Money changes so many people

Quality of life always wins in the end

BRIGHT EYES

The Lady with the multi coloured hair
is back

She has a very nice smile it brightens
up he face

She has such a dry sense of humour

She is so pretty and her presence
brightens up any day of the week

I like to see her wearing her very
distinctive makeup it shows off her
personality and individualism

DREAMS

I like her being around she is such a joyous lady

NO CONTACT

I do so miss our chats

Now we are no longer in contact my days are bereft of our days of being in contact

When I would wake from my slumber I would often check for any messages from over night

Now I feel so very empty when I don't receive a message from you

My life is devoid of any form of contact from you

DREAMS

I often wonder how you feel about not having any contact from me?

WHO KNOWS

I often wonder what would have
happened if we ever met

Would we still be in the same position
we currently find ourselves in?

Would our lives have changed for the
better?

I would hope so

But who knows

All I know is I have so many regrets

What if? Who knows

<u>QUESTIONS WITH NO ANSWERS</u>

*So why did you ever want to contact
me in the first place?*

To then not wish to meet with me?

So many questions unanswered

*Was I so naïve to have not realised you
would never agree to meet me*

*I suppose as an elderly man it was just
a dream?*

My life had been so enriched by you

DREAMS

And now I feel so empty

*But for you, life carries on and it may
have been just a game for you to play?*

*Who knows only you know the answer
to the questions*

<u>*SHARING*</u>

*I don't have much what I do have
could have bee4n shared with you*

*All I ever wanted to be was someone
who cared*

*To others it may have seemed like
being needy and wanting who knows
what it was I felt for you*

*There are many people who would
never understand how I felt for you*

*My love for you was free and without
any conditions*

<u>*LIFE*</u>

Life is made up of so many tiers and levels

If life was smooth and easy then it would be so very boring and predictable

Life isn't like a book

If it was it would be so easy

Life's journey would be so easy when in fact it so much better

Life is full of surprises

DREAMS

It certainly keeps me on my toes

HOW WELL HAVE WE DONE?

How well have we done in life, what is
the measurement of success?

To come from a city with such
depravation

Being brought up with a mother who
couldn't read or write

As children the Beano and Dandy
were our teachers

Also, the Commando comic helped in
our reading

DREAMS

Reading words such as "achtung" and "spitfeur" taught so much

It did not mean we just read comics but it helped

Now in the future we are extremely successful in our chosen professions

DREAMER

Is everyone a dreamer?

*Being a dreamer comforts one
against the real world*

*The problem with dreams they
have a habit of bursting*

*A dreamer never seems to make
a mark on the world*

*My life has become somewhat
like a dream*

Who wants to live in a dream?

DREAMS

The realities of life have a habit
of smacking a dreamer hard
across the face

No-one believes in a dreamer
because dreams never come true

IDEA

You have no idea of how I truly
feel about you

You are oblivious to my feelings
towards you

But someone of your age why
would you know about how I feel

Your body is so divine

Should I be feeling this way about
you?

Who knows because I don't

<u>NORMAL</u>

My world isn't what one would
call "normal"

I seem to wait for the
opportunity for my life to move
on

Others may feel that I am not
living a "normal" life whatever it
is?

My life in my eyes is very
"normal"

Who knows what normal exactly
means

DREAMS

Perhaps those who are "normal"
are now in the minority?

<u>*MEET*</u>

Why could you never meet with me?

You hurt me to the quick such pain

I thought I was such a fool perhaps I was who knows?

You turned my life upside down

All I ever wanted was to meet for a coffee

What was so wrong with that?

DREAMS

Because of a cup of coffee, we never met one another

As hard as I tried you refused to meet or made every excuse for not able to meet such a shame

Now look at us

Alone

<u>SOMEONE</u>

My life is full of loneliness I dream of meeting someone to make me feel whole once again

Is it too much to ask for?

I don't mean just anyone just a loving person to share our lives together

To share the ups and downs of life the upsets, the heartache and happiness

Is it too much to ask for?

DREAMS

Surely not

<u>MISTAKES</u>

Did I make a mistake in life who knows?

What have I done it all started in my twenties and has had a profound effect on me in later life

Is it time to stop thinking like that

If I carry on it could destroy everything I have

I cannot carry on thinking this way

DREAMS

*It is time to bury my mistakes
and to begin to live my life to the
full*

*Guilt is a terrible feeling it eats
away at the soul*

QUESTIONS

Who and what are you

You have never opened up to me
are you hiding a secret from me?

You gloss over my questions

You don't even know my name, it
makes me feel so angry, at not
knowing my name after so long

I am so open with you

On the other hand, you have told
me nothing about yourself

DREAMS

How sad that you have never
been open with me

Because of the way you are
towards me we will never meet

It is so so sad

<u>EVIL</u>

There are so many kind people in
the world

There are also terrible people

When we are all first born we
know nothing of this world or
about the hatred

No-one is born evil

But some are fed the drivel by
their parents

The parents then start to fill a child's mind with such hatred and racism towards others

We are all human no matter what skin colour we are born with

We are born with love pounding in our hearts and not hatred

TIME TO DREAM

Is dreaming such a weakness

I dream all the time

I sometimes hope my dreams
may come true

Who knows where my dreams
may take me

Life is such a long journey

Who knows what might be just
around the corner?

DREAMS

It is why I dream about what is just around the corner

Who knows?

<u>*NAIVITY*</u>

*Does she realise how she comes
across to others?*

She comes across as naïve

*Perhaps she isn't as naïve as she
makes out perhaps it is just a
smoke screen?*

She is so angelic

*I know not what goes through
her mind*

DREAMS

My time is not her time in life

My time is coming to an end

I have lived my life

LEARN

Do we ever learn from our
mistakes?

Of course, we don't far from it

I have made so many mistakes in
my life

And I have never learnt one
lesson from my mistakes

Have I ever learnt from my
mistakes?

The obvious answer is a resounding no!!

Will I ever learn from my mistakes?

The answer is

NO

<u>LIFE DERAILED</u>

My life is so upside down

*I no longer know where I am
heading to*

*It is so foggy and without any
direction*

*Perhaps you will help me get
back on track*

*I dream of having a loving lady
in my life*

DREAMS

I don't seem to have settled in my life I so restless

Perhaps you have derailed my journey in life

Yes you

HAPPINESS

Sat beneath a tree in the English
countryside in the full glare of
the morning sun

Rolling fields stretched for miles
further than the eye can see

Not another soul in sight it feels
so relaxing

Not everyone is so lucky to find a
spot to be able to shut out the
manic world

A world seemingly in such chaos

*People not knowing what will
happen next daring to switch on
the news in the morning*

*To be able to sit in the
countryside and to immerse into
one's thoughts is a very rare
luxury*

FIVE MINUTES

To walk out of the front door of
the house and within minutes to
be in the countryside is just so
wonderful

As a child the only countryside
were the large municipal parks
in Liverpool

But even so they were the lungs
of the city

I never take for granted the gift
of living in such beautiful
countryside surrounding the
ancient city of Winchester

*There are not many people who
are lucky to have what I have*

*Lucky is not the word to use to
have such beauty surrounding
the house I live in*

<u>RUN</u>

The world is being run by people
on the face of things don't care
for others who aren't as powerful

It was only months earlier these
people had been democratically
elected to run their countries

They forget they have been
elected by the people to serve
their people

I am afraid what has happened
the world has become so unstable
and it is frightening to see what
they are doing the "elected"

DREAMS

*Is the world on the brink of a
third world war?*

We shall see, time will tell

*A war that could destroy much
of the planet*

*But when will mother nature
takes her revenge*

On humanity

<u>SELECTIVE</u>

Do we give up dreaming as we
get older?

Or do we dream even more?

As children dreams are ten a
penny

As we grow older dreams are
more selective and targeted

As young adult's dreams are
chased some come true many do
not

DREAMS

That is until we are older never
let a dream go

Dreams do come true no matter
old a person is

And no matter what the dream
is

Made in the USA
Columbia, SC
22 June 2018